With love from:

....

You remember all of my accomplishments and forget the mistakes I make.

In difficult times you were still as wonderful as always for me.

You teach me right from wrong.

To the world you are a mother, to me you are the world.

You are my role model.

You've done an amazing job at being the mom I needed to have as a child.

You're always
a helping hand.
You'll never turn away
when I need someone.

Of all the gifts that life as offered me, a loving mother is the greatest I was given.

Your hugs always made things better.

You are my emotional support and I can always come to you when I'm stuck in life.

Thank you for providing me food. It always tastes amazing.

AMAZING
TH**O**UGHTFUL
S**T**RONG
HAPPY
WOND**E**RFUL
G**R**ACEFUL

You have ears that listen, arms that hold, love that's never ending and a heart that's made of gold.

You are a blessing no one can replace.

You loved me since I was born, but I've loved you my whole life.

As a child,
you've put me to bed
and read wonderful
stories to me.

thank you for making my days better when I am having a bad day.

_____

CPSIA information can be obtained
at www.ICGtesting.com
Printed in the USA
LVHW070310120423
744143LV00002B/7